FunTime® Piano

Christmas

Level 3A-3B

Easy Piano

This book belongs to: _____

Arranged by

Nancy and Randall Faber

Production Coordinator: Jon Ophoff
Design: Terpstra Design, San Francisco
Engraving: Dovetree Productions, Inc.

FABER
PIANO ADVENTURES®
3042 Creek Drive
Ann Arbor, Michigan 48108

A NOTE TO TEACHERS

FunTime® Piano Christmas is a delightful collection of Christmas favorites arranged for the Level 3 piano student. The selections include both traditional and popular Christmas favorites which students find especially appealing.

FunTime® Piano Christmas is part of the *FunTime® Piano* series. "FunTime" designates Level 3 of the *PreTime® to BigTime® Piano Supplementary Library* arranged by Faber and Faber.

Following are the levels of the supplementary library, which lead from *PreTime®* to *BigTime®*.

PreTime® Piano	(Primer Level)
PlayTime® Piano	(Level 1)
ShowTime® Piano	(Level 2A)
ChordTime® Piano	(Level 2B)
FunTime® Piano	(Level 3A–3B)
BigTime® Piano	(Level 4)

Each level offers books in a variety of styles, making it possible for the teacher to offer stimulating material for every student. For a complimentary detailed listing, e-mail faber@pianoadventures.com or write us at the mailing address below.

Visit **www.PianoAdventures.com**.

Helpful Hints:

1. Hands-alone practice can be very helpful in learning a piece.

2. The songs can be assigned in any order. It is often best to allow the student's interest and enthusiasm to determine the order of selection.

3. As a special project, the student may wish to tape record a selection of Christmas songs as a surprise present for parents and family.

ISBN 978-1-61677-006-8

TABLE OF CONTENTS

Jingle Bells

Music and Lyrics by
J. PIERPONT

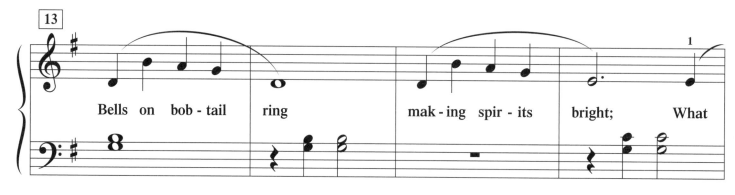

Silent Night

Music by FRANZ GRÜBER
Lyrics by JOSEPH MOHR

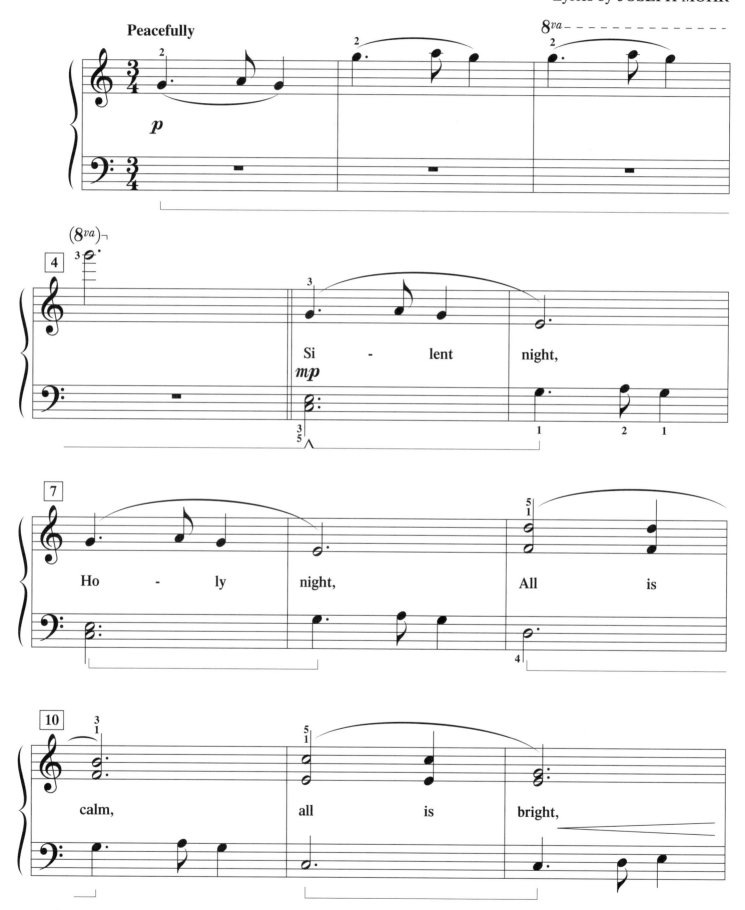

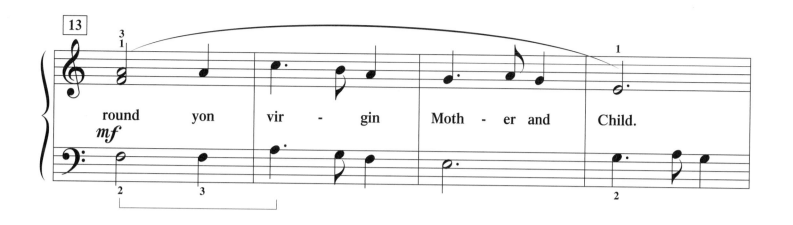

round   yon   vir   -   gin   Moth   -   er and   Child.

Ho   -   ly   In   -   fant so   ten   -   der and   mild.

Sleep   in   heav - en - ly   peace,_____

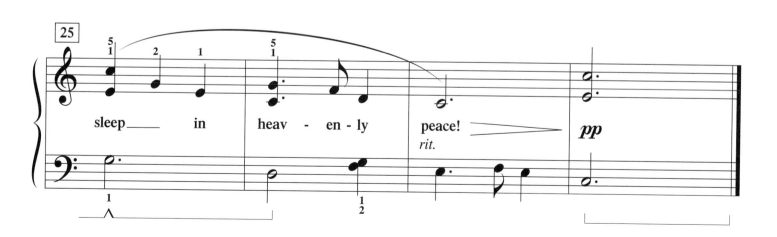

sleep_____ in   heav - en - ly   peace!
rit.

O Christmas Tree
(O Tannenbaum)

TRADITIONAL GERMAN CAROL

Deck the Halls

TRADITIONAL

Deck the halls with boughs of hol- ly, Fa la la la la, la la la la,

'Tis the sea- son to be jol- ly, Fa la la la la, la la la la,

Don we now our gay ap- par- el, Fa la la la la la la la la,

cresc.

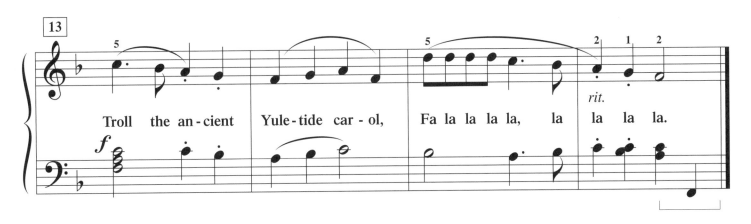

Troll the an- cient Yule- tide car- ol, Fa la la la la, la la la la.

rit.

God Rest Ye Merry, Gentlemen

TRADITIONAL

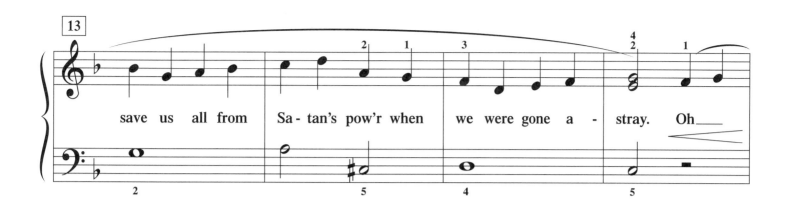

save us all from Sa - tan's pow'r when we were gone a - stray. Oh___

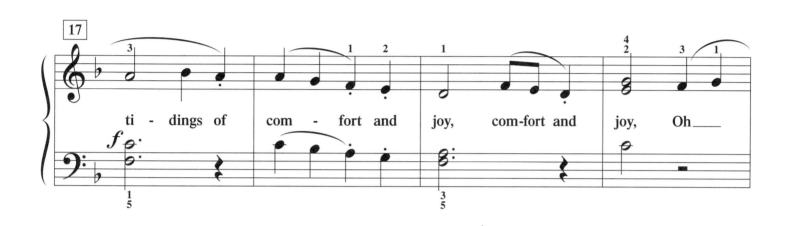

ti - dings of com - fort and joy, com-fort and joy, Oh___

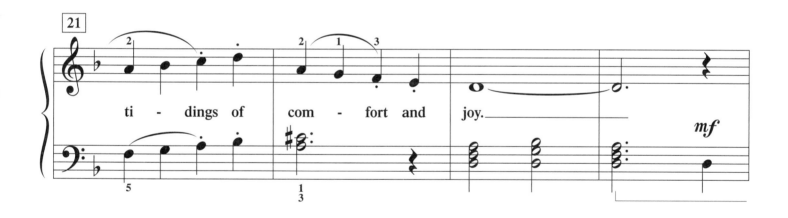

ti - dings of com - fort and joy.___

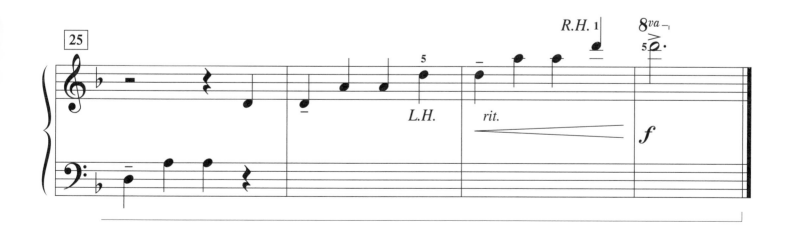

Rudolph the Red-Nosed Reindeer

Music and Lyrics by
JOHNNY MARKS

Not too fast

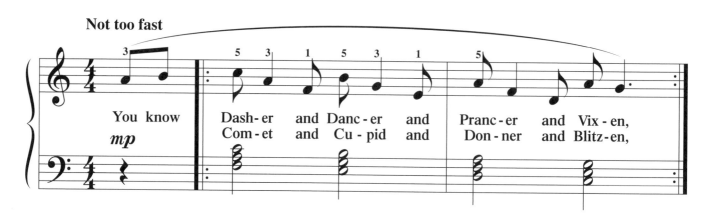

You know *mp*
Dash-er and Danc-er and | Pranc-er and Vix-en,
Com-et and Cu-pid and | Don-ner and Blitz-en,

but do you re-call | the most fa-mous rein-deer of | all? *rit.*

Happily

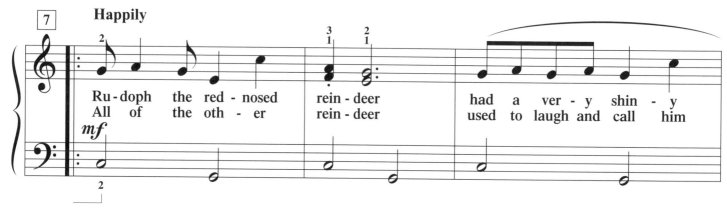

Ru-doph the red-nosed | rein-deer | had a ver-y shin-y
All of the oth-er | rein-deer | used to laugh and call him
mf

nose, | and if you ev-er | saw it,
names, | they nev-er let poor | Ru-dolph

The Night Before Christmas Song

Music by JOHNNY MARKS
Lyrics adapted by JOHNNY MARKS
From Clement Moore's Poem

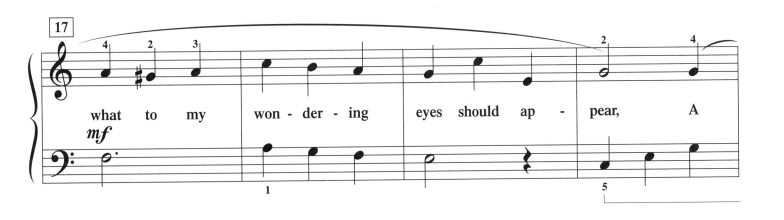

what to my won - der - ing eyes should ap - pear, A

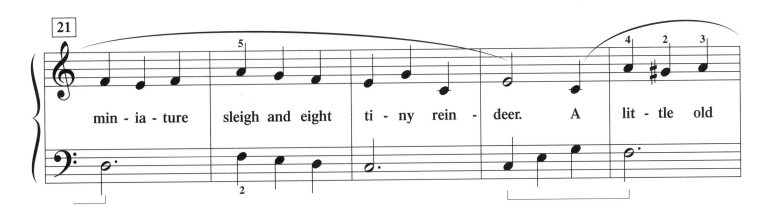

min - ia - ture sleigh and eight ti - ny rein - deer. A lit - tle old

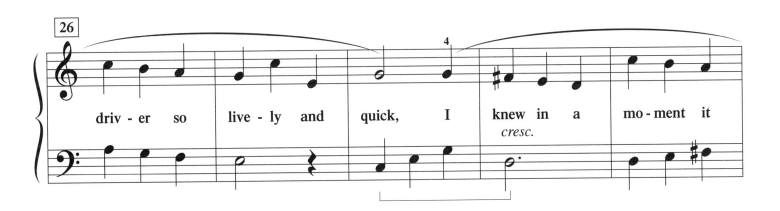

driv - er so live - ly and quick, I knew in a mo - ment it

D.S. 𝄋 al Coda

🜋 Coda

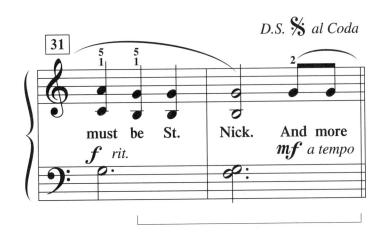

must be St. Nick. And more

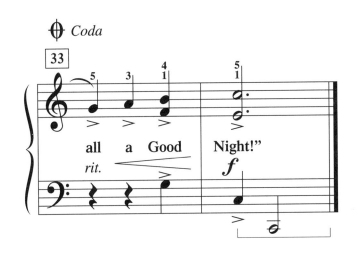

all a Good Night!"

Rockin' Around the Christmas Tree

Music and Lyrics by
JOHNNY MARKS

O Little Town of Bethlehem

Music and Lyrics by
L. H. REDNER

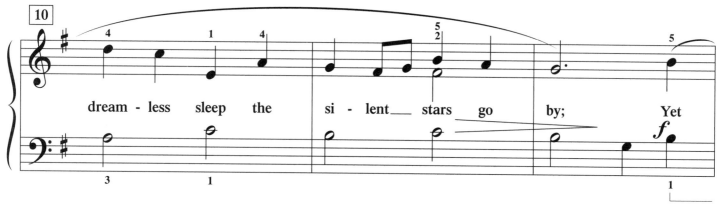

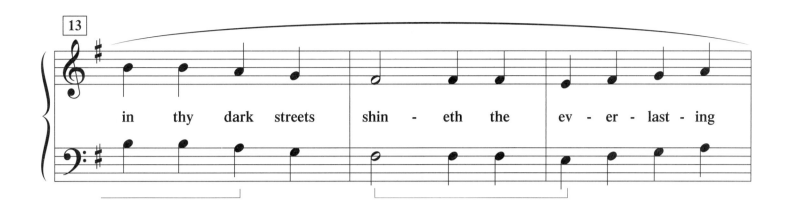

in thy dark streets shin - eth the ev - er - last - ing

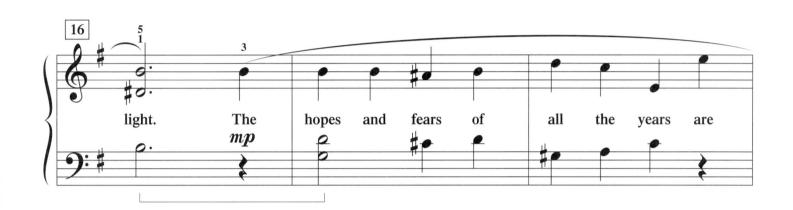

light. The hopes and fears of all the years are

mp

BOTH HANDS 8va - - - - - - - - - -

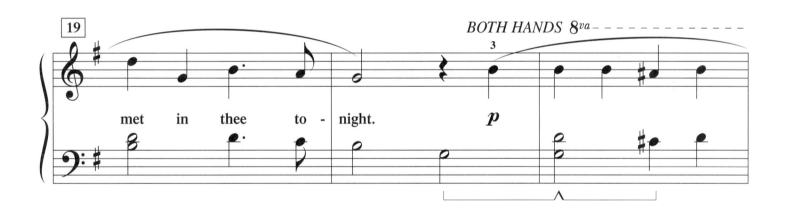

met in thee to - night.

p

(**8va**) -

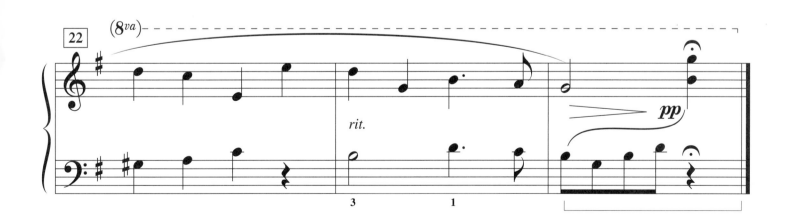

rit.

pp

FF1006

Carol of the Bells

Music by M. LEONTOVICH
Lyrics by PETER J. WILHOUSKY

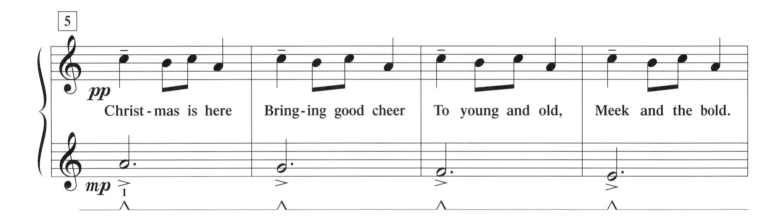

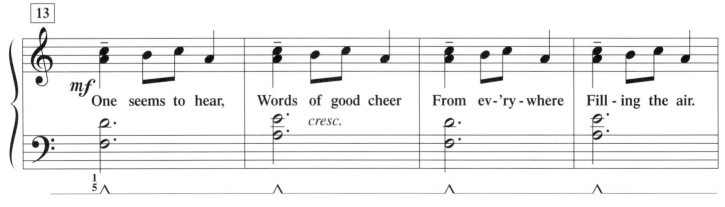

Angels We Have Heard on High

TRADITIONAL

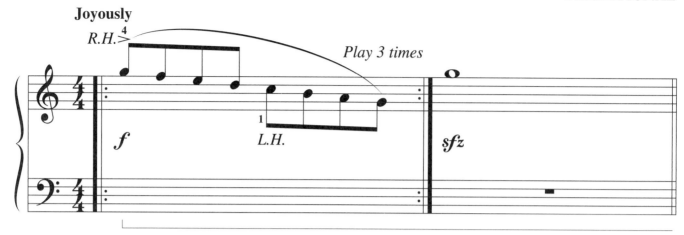

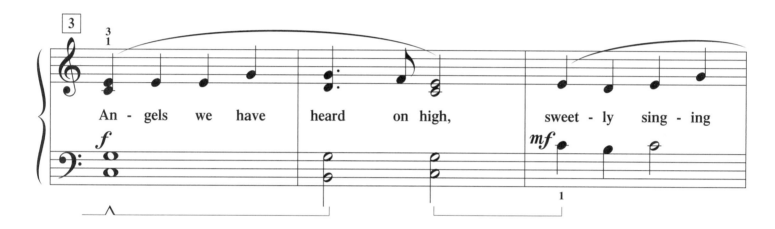

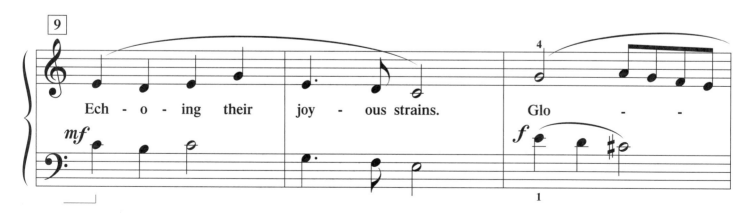

O Come, All Ye Faithful
(Adeste Fideles)

Transcribed by F. OAKELEY
WADE'S "CANTUS DIVERSI"

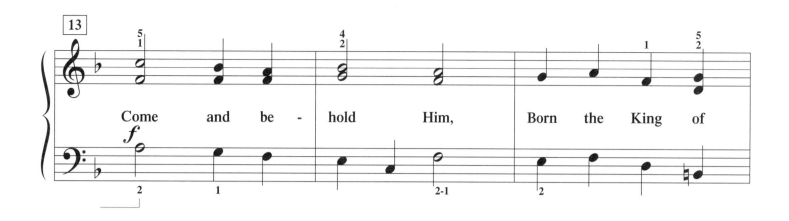

Come and be - hold Him, Born the King of

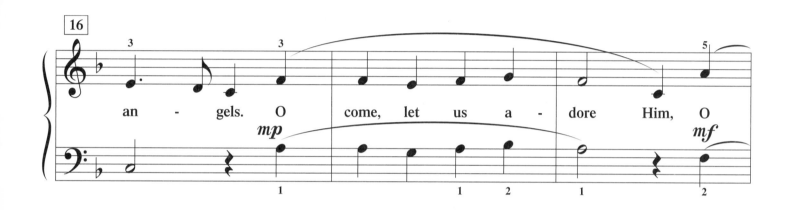

an - gels. O come, let us a - dore Him, O

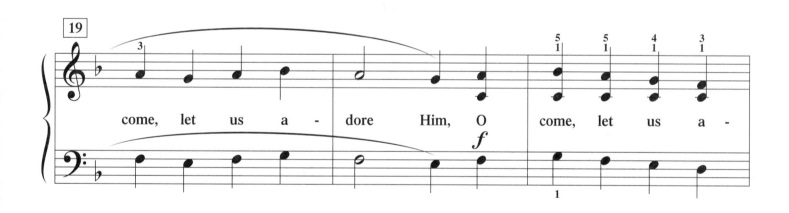

come, let us a - dore Him, O come, let us a -

dore Him;____ Christ,_____ the Lord.

I Heard the Bells on Christmas Day

Music by JOHNNY MARKS
Lyrics by HENRY WADSWORTH LONGFELLOW
adapted by JOHNNY MARKS

Let It Snow! Let It Snow! Let It Snow!

Music by JULE STYNE
Lyrics by SAMMY CAHN

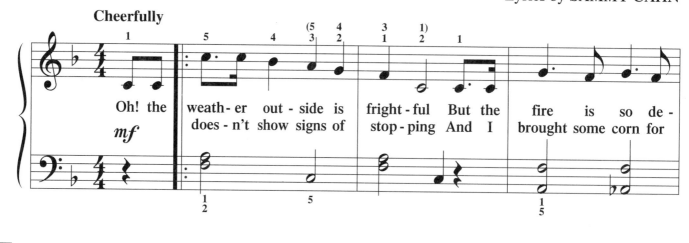

Oh! the weath-er out-side is fright-ful But the fire is so de-
does-n't show signs of stop-ping And I brought some corn for

light-ful. And the since we've no place to go, Let it
pop-ping. And The lights are turned way down low. Let it

snow! Let it snow! Let it snow! It snow! When we

fin-al-ly kiss good-night, How I'll hate go-ing out in the

storm! But if you'll real-ly hold me tight

All the way home I'll be warm. The fi-re is slow-ly

dy - ing And my dear, we're still good - bye - ing, But as

long as you love me so, Let it snow! Let it snow! Let it snow!

The Most Wonderful Day of the Year

Music and Lyrics by
JOHNNY MARKS

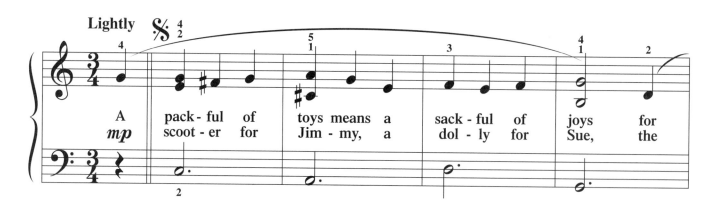

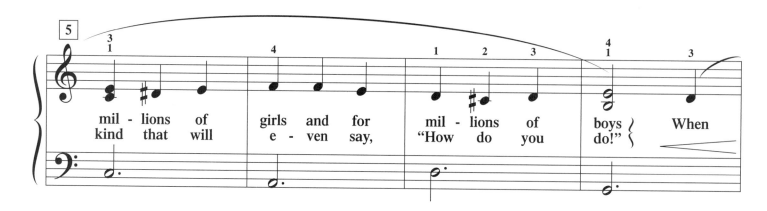

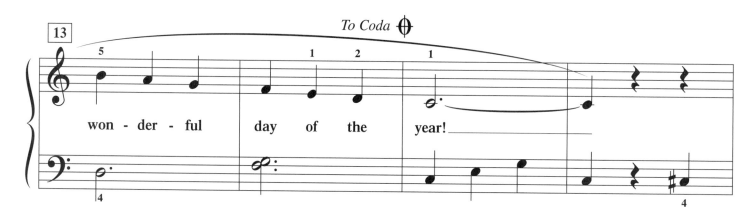

We Wish You a Merry Christmas

TRADITIONAL ENGLISH CAROL

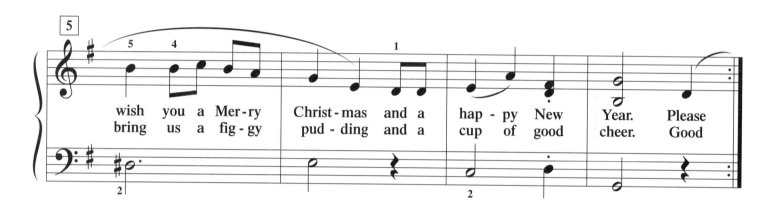

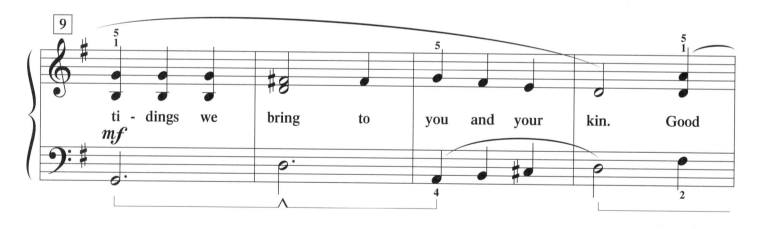

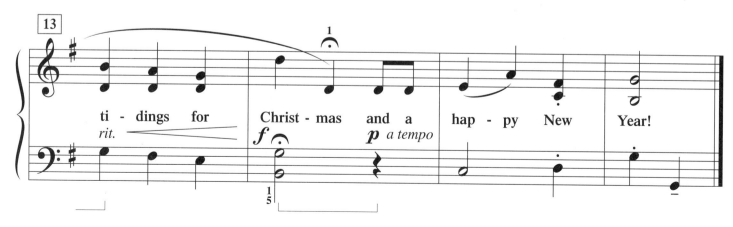